Syed Baarrij

Comprehensive Network Capacity Monitoring Guideline (GSM and UMTS)

AF153270

Syed Baarrij

Comprehensive Network Capacity Monitoring Guideline (GSM and UMTS)

A Practical Approach for Radio Engineers

LAP LAMBERT Academic Publishing

Impressum / Imprint

Bibliografische Information der Deutschen Nationalbibliothek: Die Deutsche Nationalbibliothek verzeichnet diese Publikation in der Deutschen Nationalbibliografie; detaillierte bibliografische Daten sind im Internet über http://dnb.d-nb.de abrufbar.

Alle in diesem Buch genannten Marken und Produktnamen unterliegen warenzeichen-, marken- oder patentrechtlichem Schutz bzw. sind Warenzeichen oder eingetragene Warenzeichen der jeweiligen Inhaber. Die Wiedergabe von Marken, Produktnamen, Gebrauchsnamen, Handelsnamen, Warenbezeichnungen u.s.w. in diesem Werk berechtigt auch ohne besondere Kennzeichnung nicht zu der Annahme, dass solche Namen im Sinne der Warenzeichen- und Markenschutzgesetzgebung als frei zu betrachten wären und daher von jedermann benutzt werden dürften.

Bibliographic information published by the Deutsche Nationalbibliothek: The Deutsche Nationalbibliothek lists this publication in the Deutsche Nationalbibliografie; detailed bibliographic data are available in the Internet at http://dnb.d-nb.de.

Any brand names and product names mentioned in this book are subject to trademark, brand or patent protection and are trademarks or registered trademarks of their respective holders. The use of brand names, product names, common names, trade names, product descriptions etc. even without a particular marking in this works is in no way to be construed to mean that such names may be regarded as unrestricted in respect of trademark and brand protection legislation and could thus be used by anyone.

Coverbild / Cover image: www.ingimage.com

Verlag / Publisher:
LAP LAMBERT Academic Publishing
ist ein Imprint der / is a trademark of
AV Akademikerverlag GmbH & Co. KG
Heinrich-Böcking-Str. 6-8, 66121 Saarbrücken, Deutschland / Germany
Email: info@lap-publishing.com

Herstellung: siehe letzte Seite /
Printed at: see last page
ISBN: 978-3-659-36596-6

CONTENTS

1 Preface

This guide provides a comprehensive insight into understanding, monitoring and managing the capacity of GSM/UMTS networks.

It is different from most sources of information on GSM and UMTS, as it provides a practical approach to engineers trying to measure and enhance the capacity of real-world networks.

All of the major elements and interfaces of the RAN network are analyzed comprehensively and guidelines are given to manage the capacity of the network.

Each section begins by providing an overview of the capacity elements of the GSM or UMTS network. A brief overview of each technology is provided before capacity is discussed, but it is assumed that users of this guide will have a basic understanding of the technology they are trying to monitor.

Basics of UMTS are emphasized more as compared to GSM, as in general, GSM is considered to be easier to measure, as the air interface is less complicated.

It should be noted here that although this manual strives for completeness there will always be elements and areas of capacity which will be specific to different manufacturers. In such cases the reader should refer to the OEM vendor specific documentation for clarity and use this as a guide on what to measure.

2 Acronyms and Abbreviations

The following enlists, in alphabetical order, the abbreviated terms used in this document.

A

Abis	Interface between the BTS and the BSC
AC	Admission Control
ACK	Acknowledged
AMR	Adaptive Multi Rate Speech Codec

B

BCCH	Broadcast Common Control Channel
BER	Bit Error Rate
BHCA	Busy Hour Call Attempts
BLER	Block Error Rate
BSC	Base Station Controller
BTS	Base Transceiver Station
Bps	Bits per second

C

CAC	Connection Admission Control
CCCH	Common Control Channels
CE	Channel Elements
CS	Circuit Switched
CSSR	Call Setup Success Rate
CQI	Channel Quality Index

D

DL	Downlink
DR	Directed Retry
DSPs	Digital Signal Processors

E

Ec/No	Energy per chip/Noise (Quality of 3G pilot)

F

FR	Full Rate Speech Codec
FACH	Forward Access Channel
FACH-c	FACH for control signaling
FACH-u	FACH for user data

G

GSM	Global System of Mobile Communication also called 2G

H

HR	Half Rate Speech Codec
HC	Handover Control
HSDPA	High Speed Downlink Packet Access
HSUPA	High Speed Uplink Packet Access
HS-SCCH	High Speed Shared Control Channel
HS-DSCH	High Speed Dedicated Shared Channel
HS-PDSCH	High Speed Physical Dedicated Shared Channel
HS-DPCCH	High Speed Dedicated Physical Control Channel

I

IP	Internet Protocol

L

LAC	Location Area Code
LLC	Logical Link Control Layer

M

MAC	Medium Access Control Layer
MAC-d	Medium Access Control Layer – Dedicated
MAC-hs	Medium Access Control Layer for High Speed Data
MS	Mobile Station
MOC	Mobile Originated Call
MTC	Mobile Terminated Call
MSS	Mobile Switching System
MSC	Mobile Switching Center
MTP	Message Transfer Part of SS7

N

NBAP	Node B Application Part Protocol Layer
NRT	Non Real-Time
NACK	Not Acknowledged

O

OEM	Original Equipment Manufacturer
OLC	Over Load Control

P

PCH	Paging Channel
PCU	Packet Control Unit
PDTCH	Physical Data Transport Channel
PDU	Protocol Data Unit (Signaling packets)
PDU	Payload Data Unit (User Data)
PRX	Power Received
PTX	Power Transmitted
PS	Packet Switched

Q

QAM	Quadrature Amplitude Modulation
QPSK	Quadrature Pulse Shift Keying (type of modulation scheme)

R

R99	3GPP Standard for UMTS before HSDPA
RAB	Radio Access Bearer
RAC	Routing Area Code
RACH	Random Access Channel
RB	Radio Bearer
RNC	Radio Network Controller
RRC	Radio Resource Control
RT	Real-Time
RTSL/TSL	Radio Timeslot
RTWP	Received Total Wideband Power

S

SCCP	Signaling Connection Control Part of SS7
SDCCH/SD	Standalone Dedicated Control Channel
SGSN	Serving GPRS Support Node
SRB	Signaling Radio Bearers
SS7	Signaling System 7

T

TCH	Traffic Channel for GSM
TFI	Temporary Flow Identity
TRAU	Transcoder
TRX	Transceiver (Transmitter and Receiver)
TBF	Temporary Block Flow

U

UE	User Equipment
UMTS	Universal Mobile Telecommunication Standard also called 3G or WCDMA
UL	Uplink

V

VoIP	Voice Over IP

W

WBTS	WCDMA Base Transceiver Station

1 RAN Capacity of Network

1.1 Description of Bottlenecks in 2G RAN Network

The following shows the possible areas where the capacity of the 2G network maybe restricted:

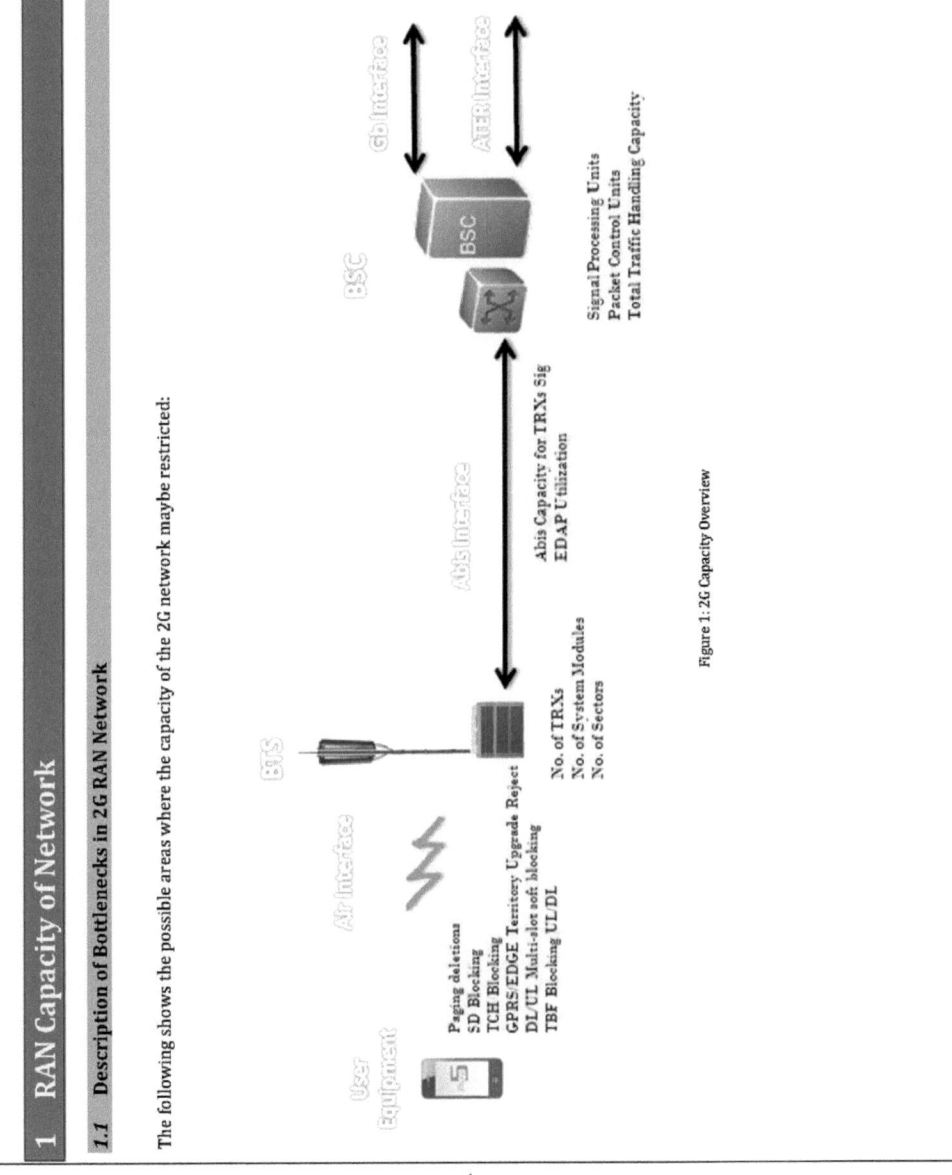

Figure 1: 2G Capacity Overview

1.2 Description of Bottlenecks in 3G RAN Network

For 3G, the following will illustrate the areas where capacity could be impacted:

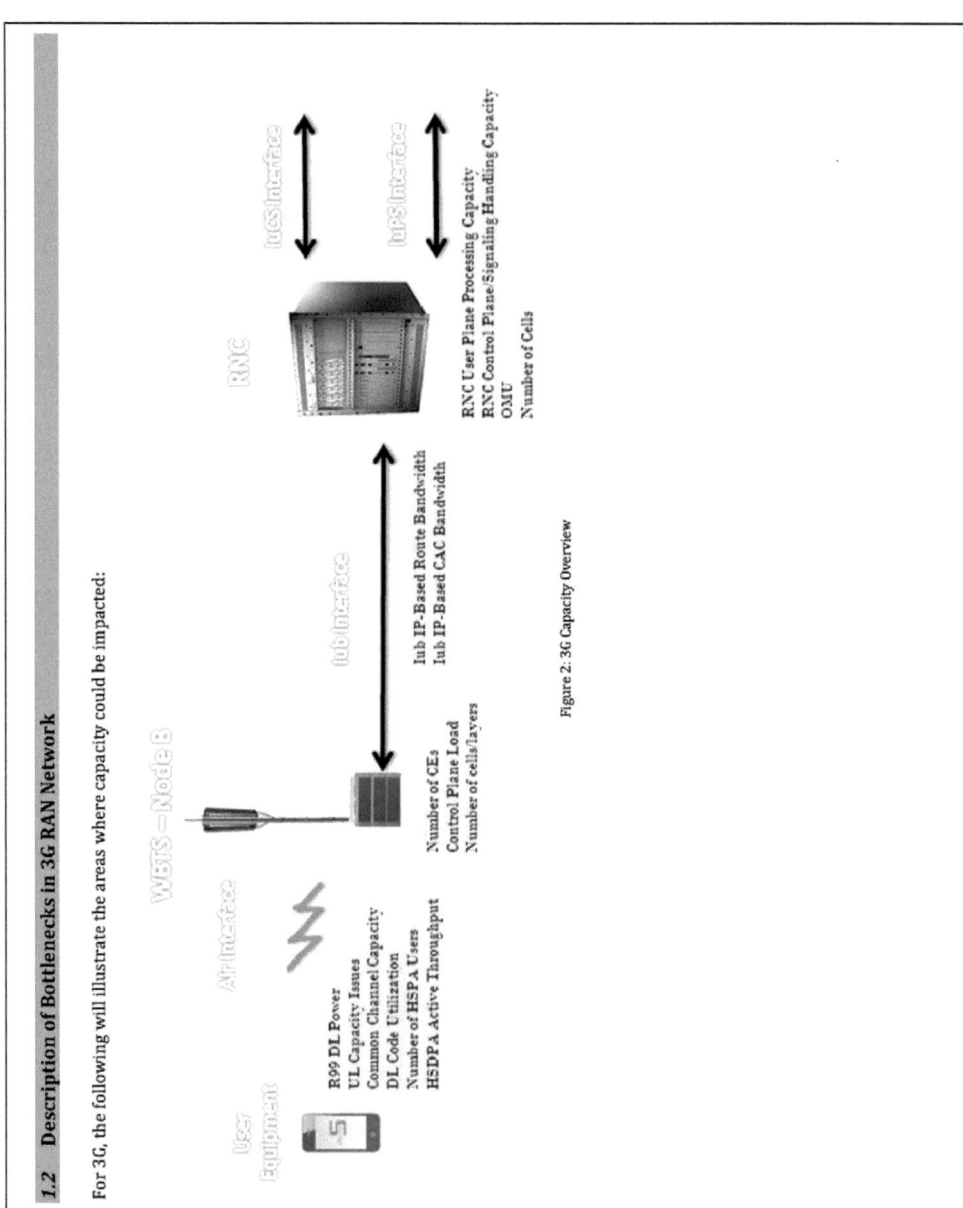

Figure 2: 3G Capacity Overview

3 RAN Capacity in 2G

3.1 2G AIR INTERFACE

Air Interface plays a pivotal role in any mobile subscriber network. It is through this interface that a subscriber is connected to the wireless network.

Capacity on the air interface for a GSM/EDGE network is affected by the following:

3.1.1 Paging Deletions

The 2G network pages the MS to establish MTC calls in a LAC. The pages are grouped together in paging groups and each MS has its own paging group that it listens to. This helps improve battery life.

The paging channel (PCH) is broadcast over the whole LAC area, the PCH channel from the A-interface is copied on Abis links of the Location Area (LA) being paged. If the LA size is too small the paging will be frequent and it will result in too many LAC boundaries, which will in turn lead to too many LAC updates and increased signaling. If the LA size is larger than what the Radio and CCCH can handle it will result in lost/deleted pages and delayed call setup.

The above applies to a CS call, PS behaves in the same manner. The paging message is sent by the MSC to the SGSN and the SGSN relays it to the BSC which in turn transmits it at appropriate times to the cells.

3.1.1.1 Indications

1. Increased paging deletions
2. Low paging success rate
3. Low CSSR

3.1.1.2 Resolution

Re-dimensioning of the affected LAC

3.1.2 SDCCH/SD blocking

The SDCCH channel is used for many signaling and transmission activities in the GSM network. It is essential for all Voice/CS call setups, Location Area Updates, IMSI Attach/Detach, SMS etc. SDCCH is a physical timeslot which is reserved on the TRX in the 2G system for this purpose.

It is very important to have sufficient capacity on the SDCCH as insufficient capacity will lead to blocking of voice calls and SMSs impacting subscribers severely.

3.1.2.1 Indications

3

1. High SD blocking
2. Low CSSR
3. Customer Complaints (Bad Subscriber Perception as call setup is rejected)

3.1.2.2   Resolution

To resolve SD Blocking and improve CSSR, the following steps should be followed.

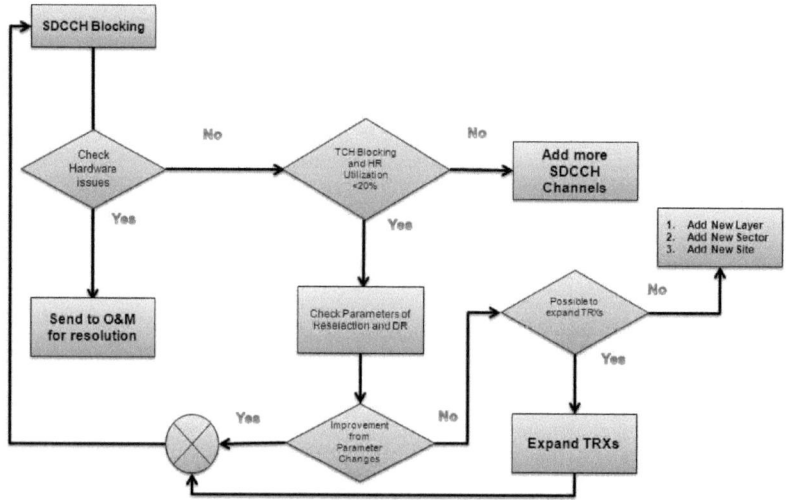

Figure 3: SD blocking Flow Chart

3.1.3   TCH blocking

The TCH or Traffic Channel in 2G carries the voice traffic of the subscribers. Like SD it is also a physical channel on a TRX in the BTS. If channels are not reserved for BCCH/SDCCH or GPRS/EDGE they are by default TCH Channels on a TRX.

One FR TCH is allocated to one voice call but the capacity on the TCH can be increased by enabling HR which increases the TCH capacity of each TSL by almost 50%. But the tradeoff is in the quality of voice as the voice codec is changed to a lower bit rate. This is improved by using Adaptive Multi Rate (AMR) voice coding.

AMR is a technique of voice coding that increases the quality and improves the error correction based on the channel characteristics. It adjusts the bit rate of the voice coder based on channel characteristics. Both AMR FR and AMR HR are supported by most handsets and OEM vendors.

But even with AMR, HR degrades the quality of speech and should not be used unless necessary.

3.1.3.1   Indications

4

1. High TCH blocking
2. Low CSSR
3. Customer Complaints (Bad Subscriber Perception as call setup is rejected)

3.1.3.2 Resolution

To resolve TCH Blocking and improve CSSR, the following steps should be followed.

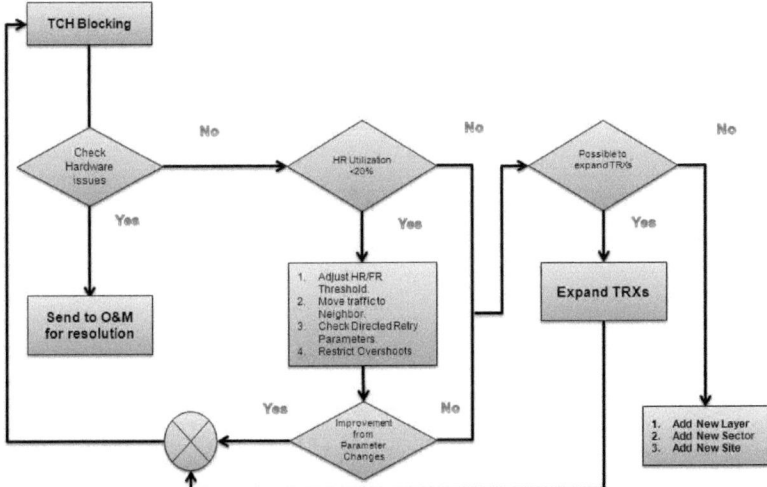

Figure 4: TCH Blocking Flow Chart

3.1.4 GPRS/EDGE Territory Upgrade Reject

GPRS/EDGE Territory is referred to as an area of TSLs in the TRXs of the system which can be assigned to subscribers for providing PS services.

It is possible to assign Dedicated GPRS/EDGE Territories i.e. an area of TSLs which will be reserved for PS services only and will not be available for voice traffic – this can cause TCH blocking on the cell.

In addition GPRS/EDGE territories can be defined which are utilized when there is no voice traffic.

This is more aptly seen below:

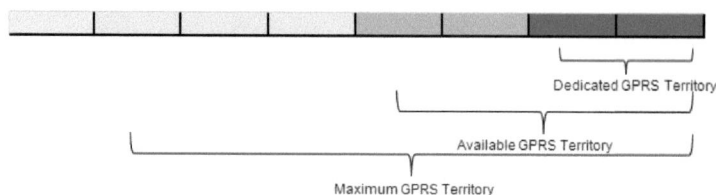

Figure 5: GPRS/EDGE Territory

When there is high demand both for voice and PS services in 2G, the voice services will have priority and PS territory is limited leading to GPRS/EDGE Territory Rejects.

3.1.4.1   Indications

1. GPRS/EDGE Territory Rejects
2. High Voice Traffic Volume and Low GPRS/EDGE Throughput
3. High PS Services

3.1.4.2   Resolution

To resolve GPRS/EDGE Territory Rejects the following flow chart is helpful:

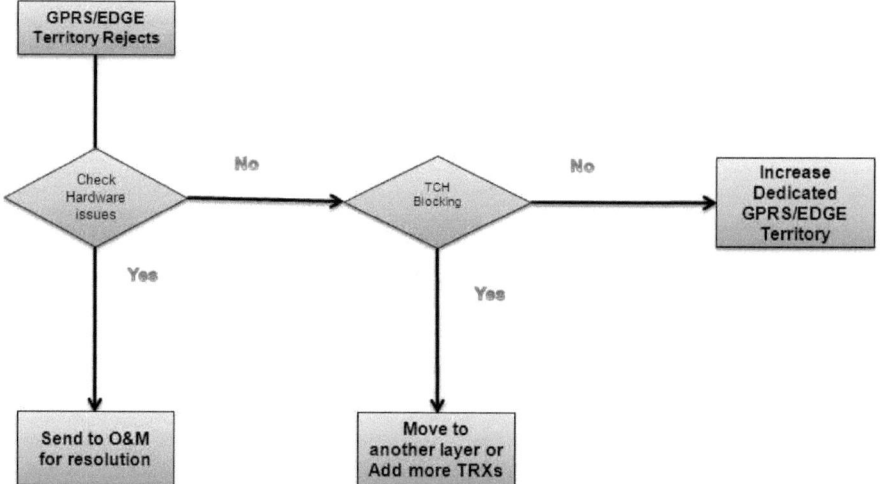

Figure 6: GPRS/EDGE Territory Rejects

3.1.5　DL/UL Multi-Slot Soft Blocking

GPRS/EDGE terminals utilize more than one TSL simultaneously in both UL and DL to improve the throughput.

The maximum timeslots that can be used in DL or UL is 8 depending on the capability of the MS or it can be a subset of 8.

The below diagram aims to explain this more clearly:

Figure 7: MS with 4xTSL in DL and 1xTSL in UL

In the above figure the MS is assigned 4xTSL in the Downlink and 1xTSL in the UL.

Other combinations not shown are also possible. When an MS capable of using Multislots either in UL or DL is restricted due to unavailability of resources then this appears as Multislot blocking.

3.1.5.1　Indications

1. High Multi-Slot Blocking
2. Low GPRS/EDGE Throughput

3.1.5.2　Resolution

To resolve DL/UL Multislot Soft Blocking the following flow chart should be used:

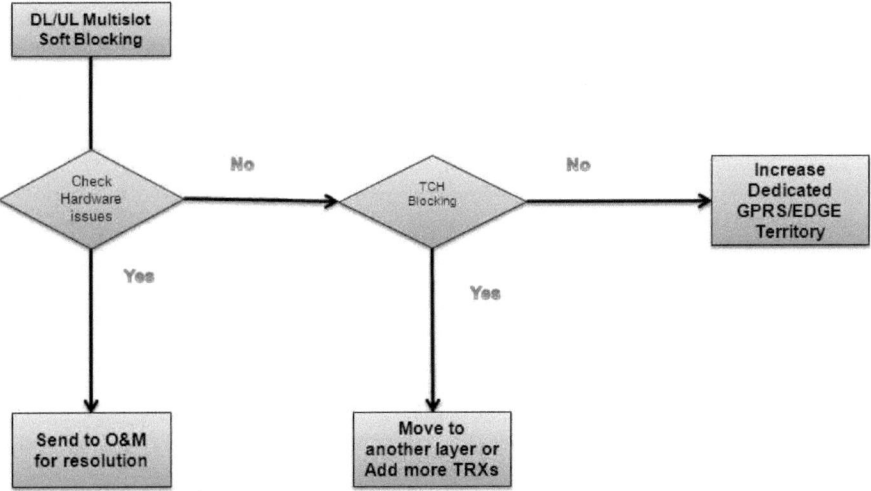

Figure 8: DL/UL Multi-slot Soft Blocking

7

3.1.6   TBF Blocking DL/UL

TBF is a physical connection to support unidirectional i.e. either UL or DL flow of LLC PDUs on PDTCH Channels. TBF is maintained for the duration of the data transfer and it is identified by its TFI.

TBF Blocking on the radio interface results when the Packet Control Unit (PCU) in the BSC tries to allocate resources and there are no resources available. This can be due to high voice calls, hardware issues or due to territory upgrade rejects.

3.1.6.1   Indications

1. High Territory Upgrade Rejects
2. High Voice Traffic Volume
3. High TCH Blocking

3.1.6.2   Resolution

Same procedures as for Section 4.1.4 and 4.1.5 should be followed to resolve TBF Blocking

3.2 2G Base Transceiver Station

The Base Transceiver Station (BTS) provides a means of communication over the air-interface between the MS/UE and the mobile network. It houses the antenna for transmitting and receiving electromagnetic waves. It connects to the BSC via the Abis Interface.

BTS comprises of a number of hardware signal processing and radio elements and they may limit the capacity of the network.

The below discusses the majority of the elements where capacity could be restricted in the BTS.

3.2.1 Number of TRXs

The transceiver is the most important unit on the air interface in a GSM network. It converts digital information in electromagnetic waves to be relayed to the antenna for transmission on the air interface.

TRX's in GSM are divided either logically or physically into 8 Radio Timeslots each if which are capable of providing full duplex functionality. Each TRX either needs to be assigned a specific frequency or it can hop over a range of frequencies. The BCCH TRX i.e. TRX having the BCCH channel cannot perform hopping and needs to transmit on a fixed frequency.

In a best case scenario one TRX can serve eight users making voice calls. As the number of users increases SD/TCH/TBF blocking appears and more TRX's are required.

The number of TRX's are limited by the frequency allocation/channels available to an operator. With an addition of TRX's the number of combining stages is increased therefore causing extra losses. TRX's can only be increased to a certain level after which a new site is required.

3.2.1.1 Indications

1. High SD blocking
2. High TCH Blocking
3. Low CSSR
4. High Multi-Slot blocking
5. High Territory Upgrade Rejects
6. Low Quality, High BER

3.2.1.2 Resolution

All steps described in section 4.1.1 need to be checked before TRXs are expanded.

3.2.2 Number of System Modules

System Modules usually provide internal and external connections to the BTS. In addition to controlling TRX's in the BTS they also store the software and provide the O&M functions for the BTS.

One System Module can support a certain number of TRX's. If TRX's in a cell/sector exceed the capacity of one system module then new system modules maybe required.

9

3.2.2.1   Indications

1.   Number of TRX's

3.2.2.2   Resolution

Manual calculation based on the number of TRX's that can be supported by the system module.

Note: This is specific to each manufacturer.

3.2.3   Number of Sectors/Cells

A typical cell site will have one or more sectors. A BTS/Site is divided into cells/sectors to improve frequency re-use and increase gain using directional antennas.

Typically each new sector consists of its own set of TRX's and antenna thereby increasing capacity. A new sector can also be added on a different layer in the same direction to relieve load on the existing sector e.g. 900 sector is congested and 1800 layer is added in the same direction as 900 sector.

A typical three sectored site is shown below:

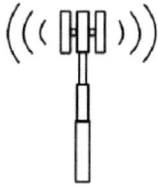

Figure 9: 3 Sectored Site

3.2.3.1   Indications

1.   Capacity required in the vicinity of the site in a different direction/layer.

3.2.3.2   Resolution

Add new TRX's and Antennas

10

3.3   2G Abis Interface

Abis is the interface between BTS and BSC and it uses LAPD protocol. Like all other interfaces it also uses a layered structure to transport information from the BTS to the BSC and vice versa.

The physical interface of the Abis is at 2048Kbit/s and each TRX TSL is either statically or dynamically mapped to it using 16Kbit/s channels.

3.3.1   Abis Capacity for TRX Signaling

Abis channels are used to carry TRX signaling information from the BTS to the BSC. They can be from 16Kbit/s to 64Kbit/s.

With the newer deployments of the Abis interface on IP this is no longer a static mapping and capacity is not limited due to statically mapped TSLs.

3.3.1.1   Indications

1. TRX signaling is high

3.3.1.2   Resolution

1. Increase allocation on Abis i.e. change from 16Kbit/s to 32Kbit/s etc.
2. Add more capacity on Abis

3.3.2   EDAP/DAP Utilization

As explained earlier Abis timeslots are divided into 16kbit/s TSL. But to provide higher data rates to EGPRS/GPRS terminals modification of the Abis is required.

This is achieved by creating a pool of 16Kbit/s TSL on the Abis which is called an Abis pool or Dynamic Abis pool.

EGPRS Dynamic Abis is either a reserved pool of 1-XX TSL on the Abis or it is allocated dynamically to any user based on the requirement.

If there are more users requesting EGPRS/GPRS services than what is allowed on the EDAP the throughput drops and substandard service is provided to the subscribers. In worst cases, it will result in high DL/UL TBF Blocking.

With the IP design of Abis this limitation will be alleviated and EDAP/DAP allocation will be dynamic. In the case of IP based Abis this will be dependent on the IP Route Bandwidth.

Below an example of EDAP allocation is shown:

			MCB	LCB
0			MCB	LCB
1				
2				
3				
4	TCH 0	TCH 1	TCH 2	TCH 3
5	TCH 4	TCH 5	TCH 6	TCH 7
6	TCH 0	TCH 1	TCH 2	TCH 3
7	TCH 4	TCH 5	TCH 6	TCH 7
8	TCH 0	TCH 1	TCH 2	TCH 3
9	TCH 4	TCH 5	TCH 6	TCH 7
10				
11				
12				
13				
14				
15	EDAP	EDAP	EDAP	EDAP
16	EDAP	EDAP	EDAP	EDAP
17	EDAP	EDAP	EDAP	EDAP
18	EDAP	EDAP	EDAP	EDAP
19	EDAP	EDAP	EDAP	EDAP
20	EDAP	EDAP	EDAP	EDAP
21	EDAP	EDAP	EDAP	EDAP
22	EDAP	EDAP	EDAP	EDAP
23				
24				
25	TRXsig1		TRXsig2	
26	TRXsig3			
27	BCFsig			
28				
29				
30				
31		Q1-management		

Figure 10: EDAP Allocation/Reservation (Courtesy of NSN)

The above is an example of statically mapped E1. It shows the mapping of the TCH TRX timeslots to the Abis. Also, shown in the figure are the timeslots reserved for TRX signaling and the EDAP.

3.3.2.1   Indications

1. Low Throughput
2. High Multi-Slot blocking
3. Territory Upgrade Rejects
4. TBF Blocking

3.3.2.2   Resolution

1. For statically mapped E1, increase EDAP TSLs
2. Add another E1.

3.4   2G Base Station Controller

2G BSC implements the digital processing functionality of the system and it provides controlling functions for all sites connected to it and on the other side it connects to the MSC.

The main functions of the BSC are listed below:

1. Handover Control
2. Power Control
3. Channel Management
4. Channel Coding/Decoding etc.

All these functions are performed by Digital Processing Units in the BSC and they are limited by the number of functions they can perform simultaneously.

The following elements limit capacity on the BSC:

3.4.1   Signal Processing Units

The signal processing unit usually implements the functionality of power control and handover control for voice channels on the air-interface.

It also implements MTP and SCCP parts of SS7 on the A-interface. Therefore it provides inter-connection between the Abis and the A-interface.

One Signal processing unit can handle a certain number of TRX's and a certain volume of traffic. When the processor load increases beyond the traffic – blocking is experienced in the form of rejection of connections.

The typical indications and resolution for such cases is provided below:

3.4.1.1   Indications

1. Processor load increases to more than 90%

3.4.1.2   Resolution

1. Add more DSP cards
2. Shift sites from the overloaded DSP card
3. Shift sites to other unloaded BSCs
4. Add a new BSC

3.4.2   Packet Control Units

The PCU implements the functionality to provide GPRS/EDGE Processing to the BSC. It is usually part of the Signal Processing Unit. It implements Packet Abis and Packet Gb functions and provides radio connection establishment and management procedures.

Each PCU is also limited by the number of EDAP pools and Radio Territories it can handle. The capacity of the PCU is heavily dependent on the manufacturers and documentation should be consulted to ensure correct dimensioning and monitoring.

The following provides a generic guideline to monitoring and resolving PCU related capacity issues:

3.4.2.1   Indications

1. High UL/DL EDAP Congestion due to PCU limitations
2. High PCU Utilization

3.4.2.2   Resolution

1. Shift sites from loaded to unloaded PCU
2. Add more PCU cards

3.4.3   Total Traffic Handling Capacity of the BSC

The BSC has a total traffic handling capacity after which the BSC will start rejecting connections and start implementing overload control.

This is defined both in BHCA and in Erlang. The traffic on the BSC should never exceed 80% of the total traffic handling capacity of the BSC.

3.4.3.1   Indications

1. High traffic on the BSC

3.4.3.2   Resolution

1. Add more DSP cards
2. Shift sites from the overloaded DSP card
3. Shift sites to other unloaded BSCs
4. Add a new BSC

4   RAN Capacity in 3G

4.1   Basics of 3G

Unlike 2G that uses multiple frequencies, 3G only uses one frequency and utilizes CDMA to separate users, cells and channels?

The packet handling and transfer is much more complicated and advanced. In modern networks the 3G transport is completely IP based which complicates matters – when measuring capacity.

With the introduction of smart phones the factors affecting capacity have increased and they need to be addressed appropriately.

The following sections attempt to briefly but clearly elaborate on factors affecting 3G RAN and explain how to analyze them and relieve congestion.

For document completeness some concepts of 3G are briefly discussed in this document. It should although be noted that this guide focuses on the capacity limiting factors in 3G. For a detailed discussion of the other concepts of 3G refer to [1] or [6]

4.1.1   Common Channels and Capacity

Common Channel Capacity refers to the capacity of the Channels in DL or UL which are shared by multiple users.

In 3G the channels are mapped to transport and then to logical channels, a mapping of both UL and DL channels is shown below:

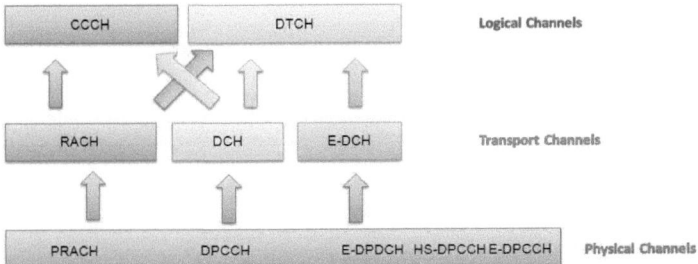

Figure 11: UL Channel Mapping

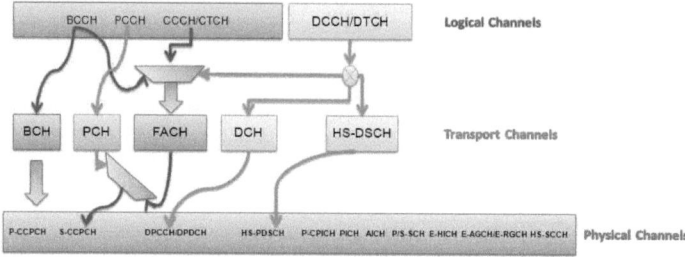

Figure 12: DL Channel Mapping

The capacity on the common channels can be restricted on the following channels:

UL:

- RACH

DL:

- FACH
- PCH

Steps to analyze and address capacity on these channels are described in section 5.2. For a detailed description refer to [9].

4.1.2   RRC Connected Modes

In UMTS more focus is given to Packet Switched Data and efficient resource utilization is required. With the introduction of short message services over packet data and numerous other background applications requiring instant short-bursts of data it became even more pertinent to develop more effective solutions to manage UE battery life, reduce signaling load and improve subscriber perception.

This lead to the introduction of RRC Connected Modes where the UEs have a Radio Connection to the RNC on *common channels* or on *dedicated channels*.

The four packet states defined in the RRC connected mode state are: CELL_DCH, CELL_FACH, CELL_PCH and URA_PCH.

The state machine transition between these states is shown below:

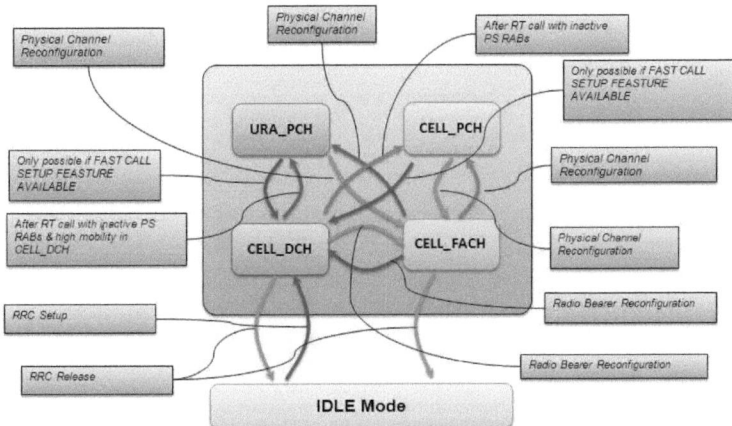

Figure 13: RRC States and Transitions

IDLE Mode: The UE does not have any connection to the RNC and only listens to the paging messages. The location of the UE is only known at the Location Area Level.

CELL_PCH: The UE has an RRC connection and listens to the paging indications and the paging messages. The location of the UE is known at cell level where the Cell_Update was performed in CELL_FACH State. The power consumption of the UE is exactly the same as in IDLE mode but the UE can be transferred to the CELL_FACH state with very less signaling, if there is a data requirement.

Transfer to CELL_DCH directly is also possible, if this feature is supported and implemented by the equipment manufacturer. e.g. in NSN it is call FAST CALL SETUP

CELL_FACH: The UE has an RRC connection and it can transfer data using the FACH and RACH channels. This state is used for transferring signaling messages and small amoounts of data. The UE can send UL data using the RACH channel and receive DL Data on the FACH channel.

In CELL_FACH state the location of the UE is known at cell level by the RNC.

In the case that the data request exceeds a certain limit, the UE requests dedicated resources and it can be transferred to CELL_DCH state with very less signaling.

With the introduction of HS-FACH and HS-RACH features, a larger amount of data can be transferred on common channels, instead of switching the UE to CELL_DCH, thereby reducing the number of UEs in CELL_DCH state.

CELL_DCH: The UE has dedicated resources allocated to it, both in UL and DL. The battery consumption is high and larger amounts of data or RT sessions are in progress. As soon as inactivity is detected, the UE is transferred to CELL_FACH or CELL_PCH to save battery life and free up dedicated resources.

4.1.3 Packet Scheduler

Packet Scheduler is the name given to the hardware which schedules packets in each TTI for packet data sessions. The TTI can be 10ms for R99 and it is fixed to 2ms for HSDPA.

For HSUPA both 10ms and 2ms TTI durations are supported.

The following scheduling modes are available:

Round Robin: The UEs are scheduled over each TTI sequentially – in a queue-like manner. This ensures equal distribution of resources amongst users.

Proportional Fair Scheduler: The type of scheduling tries to maximize the relative channel quality and throughput. Therefore subscribers with good channel conditions or the users with little throughput in the past are prioritized.

As should be inferred from above the users are time-multiplexed to use the codes of SF16 in HSDPA by the packet scheduler. This allows for the system to allocate more codes per TTI to each user.

For a detailed description, refer to [6] and [8]

4.1.4 HSDPA Channels

HSDPA uses HS-DSCH, HS-SCCH in DL and HS-DPCCH in UL for transfer of user data and control information.

HS-DSCH: Mapped to the physical HS-PDSCH channel, it carries the user information in each TTI.
HS-SCCH: Carries the de-spreading, modulation, UE Identity and HARQ information. More than one HS-SCCHs are required if code multiplexing is implemented in the BTS.
HS-DPCCH: Carries uplink HARQ ACKs control information and reports CQI.

For further information refer to [9] and [10]

4.1.5 Code multiplexing

The packet scheduler can schedule more than one user per TTI if the current users have not consumed HS-SCCH, HS-PDSCH and power resources. This requires that the cell is configured with more than one HS-SCCH channel.

Each additional user in a TTI requires its own HS-SCCH channel for control information. A cell can be configured up to a maximum of 4x HS-SCCH codes, i.e. that each cell can have a maximum of 4x users simultaneously in a TTI.

Depending on the packet scheduler and whether it is dedicated or shared, the number of users and throughput thresholds can be set.

4.1.6   Multi-code use in HSDPA

HSDPA allows multi-code use to the capable UEs. This means that up to 15 SF16 codes can be simultaneously assigned to a UE depending on its capability.

All 16 SF16 codes cannot be used for HSDPA as at least one code is required for signaling.

In addition codes are required from the code tree for RT services and other control channels. Most manufacturers allow multiple combinations of codes which can be allocated like 5, 8, 10, 12, 14, 15 etc. this allows multiple users to access the HSDPA service.

If HSDPA is enabled in a cell, 5 codes by default are reserved for HSDPA.

Air or Um Interface in 3G is more complex than in 2G. It requires an in-depth understanding and analysis of a myriad of different factors before a cell can be labeled as congested.

The capacity limiting factors on the 3G air interface are given below:

4.2.1   R99 Downlink Power

Downlink Power for a BTS is a limited resource and it is distributed according to requirements amongst common/dedicated channels.

The downlink power transmitted increases with the increase in number of UEs. *Ptxtarget* is the value defined for the downlink power of the cell which should not be exceeded; otherwise, the RNC starts the overload control.

Before admitting each RT RAB in the cell, the RNC estimates the increase in total transmission power and evaluates whether allowing it will take the cell into overload area. If that is the case then the request is rejected due to DL power limitation by admission control (AC).

The load areas for R99 downlink power are shown below:

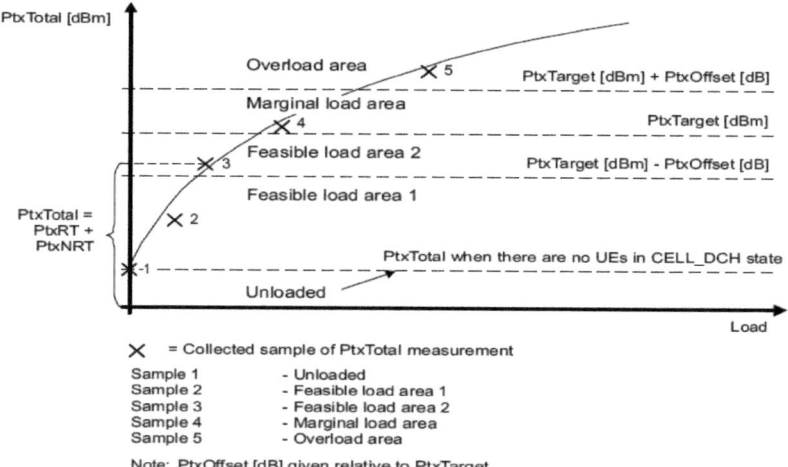

Figure 14: R99 Downlink Power Classes (Courtesy of NSN)

4.2.1.1   Indications

1. RRC Setup Rejections due to AC
2. Service Rejections/Pre-emptions

20

4.2.1.2   Resolution

1. Increase PA power
2. Adjust Parameter settings for *Ptxtarget, PtxOffset etc.*
3. Control Overshooting
4. Check SHO Overhead and optimize
5. Add 2nd/3rd Carrier or a new site

4.2.2   UL Capacity Issues

As discussed, WCDMA code multiplexes users on a single frequency. Each user transmits certain power on the same frequency and this leads to an increase in background interference.

If not managed properly the cell starts breathing and the coverage of the cell reduces i.e. Admission Control starts rejecting connections.

The UL codes in WCDMA are not orthogonal and UEs interfere with each other, increasing the noise levels.

The capacity of the WCDMA system is directly proportional to the level of interference and amongst interference the biggest contributor is UL noise.

The *Received Total Wide-band Power (RTWP) or Prxtotal* in a cell represents the total noise in the cell.

The following illustrates the areas of load in uplink:

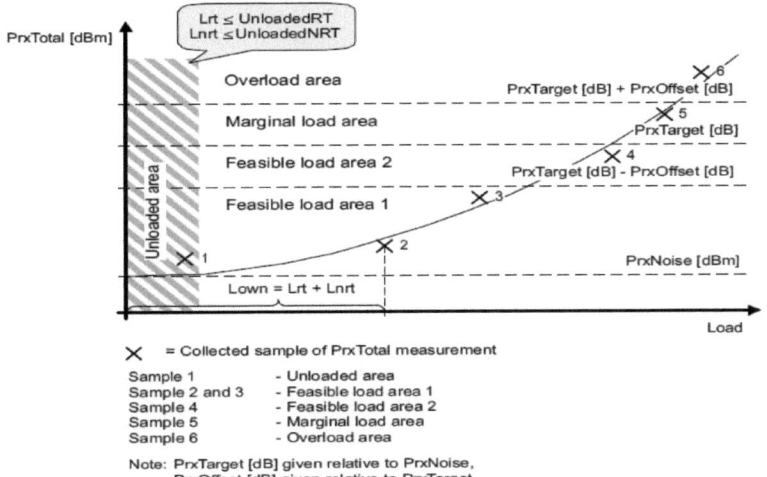

Figure 15: Prxtotal load Areas (Courtesy of NSN)

UL power or interference issues are predominantly due to the following reasons:

21

- Incorrect parameter settings
- Missing neighbors
- Hardware or software issues
- UE behavior
- Too much network allocated traffic

4.2.2.1   Indications

1. High UL Load/Interference
2. Service Rejections
   a. RB Rejections
   b. SRB Rejections
   c. HSDPA Rejections due to UL DCH

4.2.2.2   Resolution

The following flow diagram provides methods and techniques that can be used to resolve RACH overload:

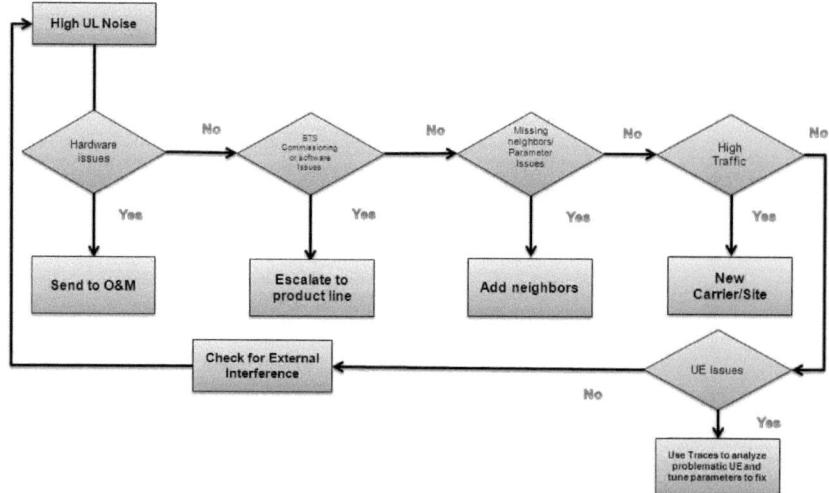

Figure 16: UL Noise Analysis

Notes: The parameters that can be changed to improve the UL Interference could be numerous. The following should only serve as a guideline, on what could be checked:

Power Parameters: *PrxNoise, PrxTarget, PrxTargetPS, PrxLoadMargins etc.*
PRACH Parameters: *PRACH Preambles Power Settings, AICH Power*
HSDPA UL Return Channel Activity Settings: *Lower the activity factors for each service as this will reduce the estimated load*
UL SIR Setting: *Change the UL SIR Settings for UL DPCCH*

RRC Wait Times: *Can be revised based on field experiences, to reduce the load due to RRC Re-attempts*

4.2.3 RACH Channel Capacity

The RACH transport channel is mapped to the PRACH physical channel as shown in figure 15. The capacity of this channel is dependent on the number of users simultaneously making use of it. It is used by UEs to gain access to the network and the access attempt is called a PRACH preamble.

The RACH can also be used for control plane data (signaling) RACH-c or user plane data RACH-u. The RACH-u is used in CELL_FACH state.

If there is excessive PRACH signaling on the cell then PRACH preambles will be lost and the UE will not be able to gain access to the network. Therefore the number of acknowledged PRACH preambles per Radio Resource Report period needs to be monitored.

As for the RACH-u, if there is excessive user plane traffic then thresholds to trigger from CELL_FACH to CELL_DCH can be revised to move UEs to dedicated state and reduce load on RACH.

4.2.3.1 Indications

1. High Average PRACH preamble load
2. High RACH throughput

4.2.3.2 Resolution

1. Add more PRACH preamble signatures
2. Add more PRACH access slots
3. Add more PRACHs
4. Review parameters for transition from Cell_FACH to CELL_DCH
5. Add new carrier

4.2.4 Paging Channel (PCH) Capacity

The PCH carries the paging information and is mapped to the physical SCCPCH, refer to figure 16. There can be up to 3xSCCPCHs defined in a cell depending on the configuration of the particular cell.

The throughput capacity of the PCH channel is dependent on the number of SCCPCH channels configured and because of the code tree limitations, this also affects the number of codes allocated to HSDPA (for a discussion on code tree refer to [1])

In UMTS there are two types of paging messages i.e. Paging Type 1 and Paging Type 2. Paging Type 1 message is used in IDLE and CELL_PCH states whereas Paging Type 2 is used in Cell_DCH and Cell_FACH states.

The PCH channel capacity is only affected by the Paging Type 1 message as Paging Type 2 is carried on SRBs.

When only one SCCPCH is configured in the cell, then PCH has priority over FACH channels and due to excessive paging this may result in FACH requests being discarded. Therefore FACH load should be monitored in parallel with paging messages if one SCCPCH is configured.

Paging congestion can result from bad LAC planning, high traffic etc. This can result in lost pages and bad subscriber perception of the network.

The number of pages carried by the PCH channel on SCCPCH depends on its configuration and OEM vendor implementation.

The method of monitoring the load on the PCH channel and its resolution is given below:

4.2.4.1   Indications

1. High Number of Paging Messages
2. Lost paging messages
3. Overload on FACH-c/FACH-u

4.2.4.2   Resolution

The following flow diagram provides methods and techniques that can be used to resolve PCH/Paging overload:

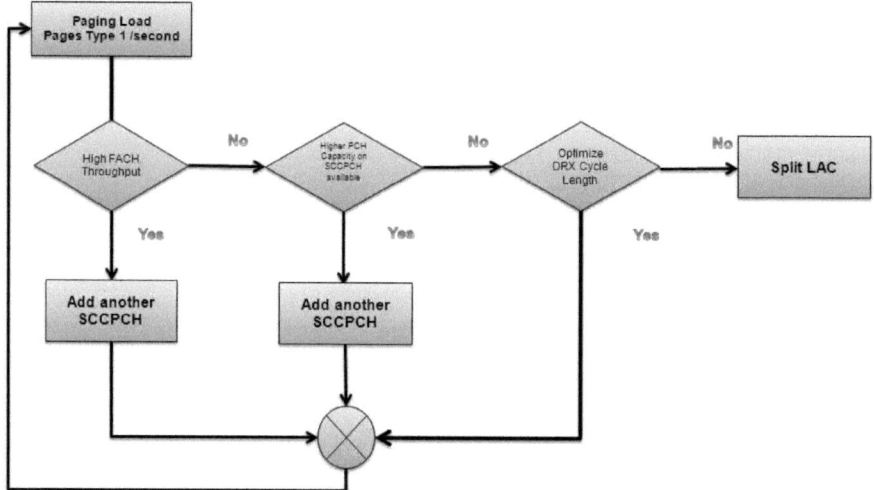

Figure 17: Paging Load Optimization

4.2.5   Forward Access Channel (FACH) Load

FACH is also carried by the SCCPCH channel on the physical layer. The FACH can also be sub-divided in FACH-c and FACH-u for control and user plane respectively.

24

FACH is used in CELL_FACH state for carrying control and user plane data. It is also affected by the configuration of the SCCPCH and the paging load, if SCCPCH is shared with PCH.

High FACH load should be monitored and remedial actions taken to resolve FACH congestion.

4.2.5.1   Indications

1.   High FACH load/throughput

4.2.5.2   Resolution

The following flow diagram provides methods and techniques that can be used to resolve FACH overload:

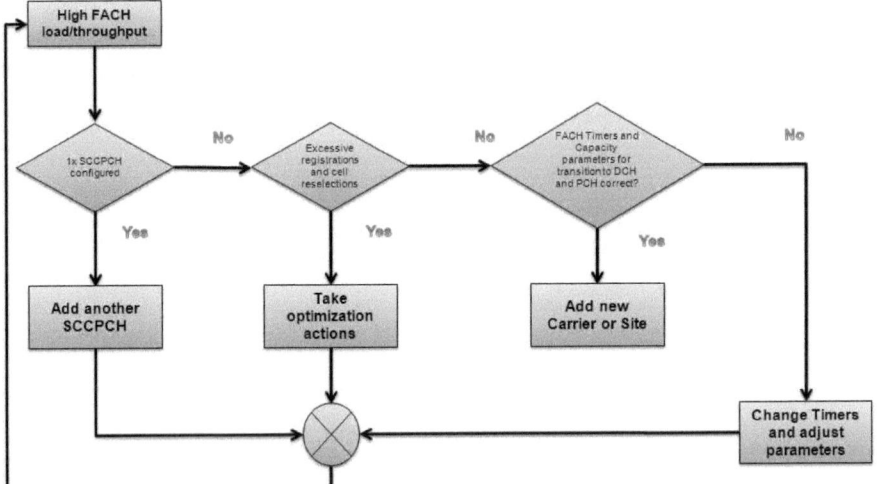

Figure 18: FACH Load Optimization

4.2.6   DL Code Tree Usage

UMTS uses both channelization and scrambling codes to provide services to its users. The DL channelization codes are used to distinguish services and DL scrambling codes are used to separate cells.

Channelization Codes are not limited in the UL, therefore there is no capacity consideration for UL codes.

The user data is spread by a channelization code from the code tree and it is a limited resource. The number of chips used to spread the user data is called the spreading factor.

25

The spreading factor is used to distinguish between different services. If a higher code is assigned for a service the code tree is essentially cut-off from that point and subsequent branches are not usable, as these codes have bad autocorrelation properties.

For a detailed discussion on codes, spreading factors and code trees please refer to a guide on UMTS Radio Interface.

HSDPA uses SF16 to provide services to the UEs. Therefore, a certain number of codes of SF16 need to be blocked for use by the HSDPA terminals. The lowest value possible is 5xSF16 codes for HSDPA.

The code tree at at SF16 is shown below:

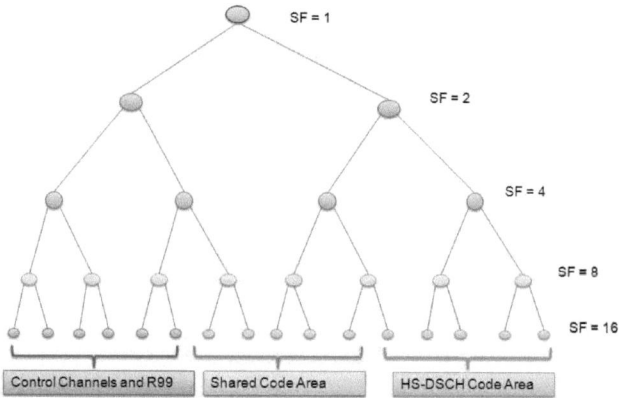

Figure 19: Typical Code Tree at SF16

For R99 services the Packet Scheduler, based on certain parameters and timers attempts to periodically upgrade the RB to a higher data rate to improve the end-user throughput. If such upgrade requests are blocked due to limited codes on that specific spreading factor it is in some OEM vendor implementations seen as blocking for the spreading factor in the code tree. These requests may get blocked due to power, code or other issues. From a practical end-user and engineering prespective this should not be taken as blocking as the user still has a connection and is able to send and receive data, albeit at a lower rate.

A typical DCH RB upgrade attempts by a packet scheduler is depicted below:

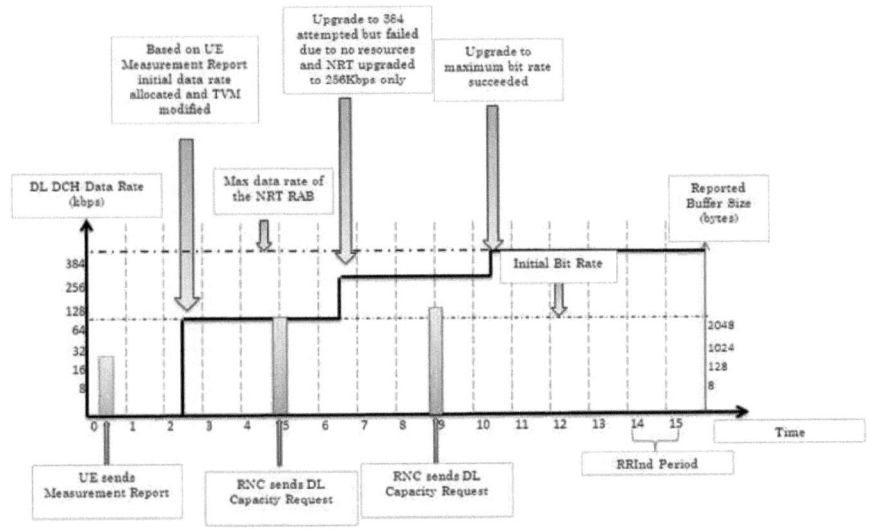

Figure 20: Upgrades of an NRT DCH by Packet Scheduler (Courtesy of NSN)

Based on the above discussion it should be noted that to consider code blocking not all the spreading factors should be taken into account. As with static HSDPA code allocation and R99 NRT RB upgrades/downgrades, code blocking on all SFs will provide an inaccurate depiction of the code tree utilization.

Therefore it is only meaningful, to calculate code blocking at SF128 and SF256, the spreading factors used by control channels and AMR Voice RBs. Code blocking for HSDPA should be calculated using other means and this document will elaborate on this subject in detail in section 5.2.7

4.2.6.1   Indications

1. High Code blocking on SF128 and SF256

4.2.6.2   Resolution

27

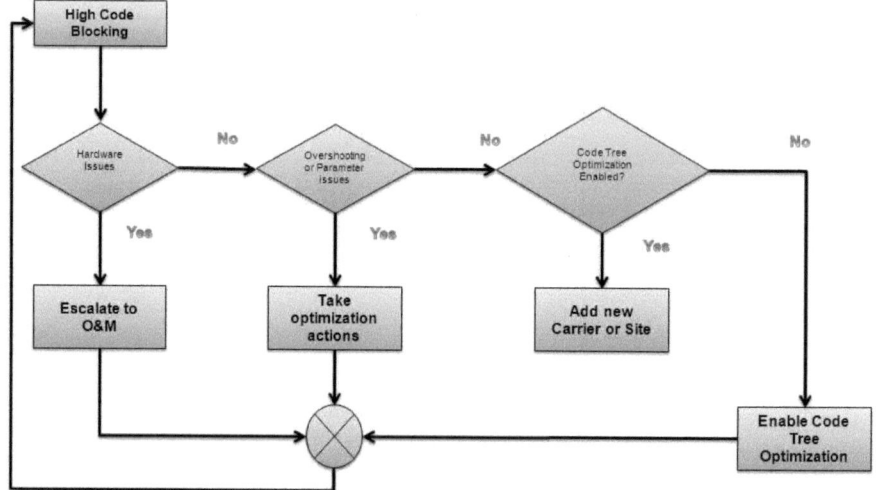

Figure 21: Code Blocking Resolution

The following parameters could be changed to improve Code Blocking in cases shown by the flowchart:

HSDPA Code Allocation: If the number of SF128 codes available is less than a certain limit, HS-PDSCH codes can be downgraded.
Number of HS-SCCH Codes: The number of HS-SCCH can be changed to reduce code tree usage but it will impact HSDPA Capacity.

Other parameters specific to each manufacturer should also be considered.

4.2.7   Number of HSPA Users

As discussed in section 5.1 multiple users can be scheduled in one TTI by the packet scheduler. However with data in the buffer for each user and with the increase in number of users, there aren't enough HS-SCCHs, HS-PDSCH and power to serve all users at once and they are scheduled in different TTIs, i.e. time-multiplexing. Now if there is an increase in duration of data in buffer for each user the throughput drops degrading subscriber performance.

Most packet schedulers allow more than 50+ users to connect to it simultaneously. If a shared packet scheduler is considered, i.e. packet scheduler shared by three or more cells of a site then due to HS-SCCH limitations the maximum simultaneous users per TTI can be 12. If however time multiplexing is considered then this KPI alone cannot give an accurate indication of the HSDPA capacity of the network as some users might be in connected state but have no data in the buffer. Such users will not impact the throughput adversely.

Thus, this KPI should be used in conjunction with **HSDPA Active Throughput** and **HSDPA Active End User Throughput** to determine whether throughput is limited due to too many users.

In addition another indication of low HSDPA throughput comes from the number of PS NRT DCHs allocated to HSDPA capable UEs due to congestion on HSDPA. This congestion can be due to high number of active users, HS-SCCH limitations and code or power issues.

The best way to measure the HSDPA throughput limitations is to use a number of KPIs as mentioned above to get an accurate indication of where and what is limiting the throughput of HSDPA Users.

Moreover the remedial actions do not necessarily mean that the site needs to be upgraded or a new site planned. There could be overshooting or parameter issues which need to be rectified first before decisions are taken to add new layers or sites.

For a discussion of HSDPA Throughput, please refer to section 5.2.8

4.2.7.1   Indications

1. High number of HSDPA Users
2. Low HSDPA Active/End User Throughput
3. DCH selected to maximum HSDPA users

4.2.7.2   Resolution

The following summarizes the discussion above and provides a systematic flow to detect HSDPA throughput limitations due to high HSDPA Users:

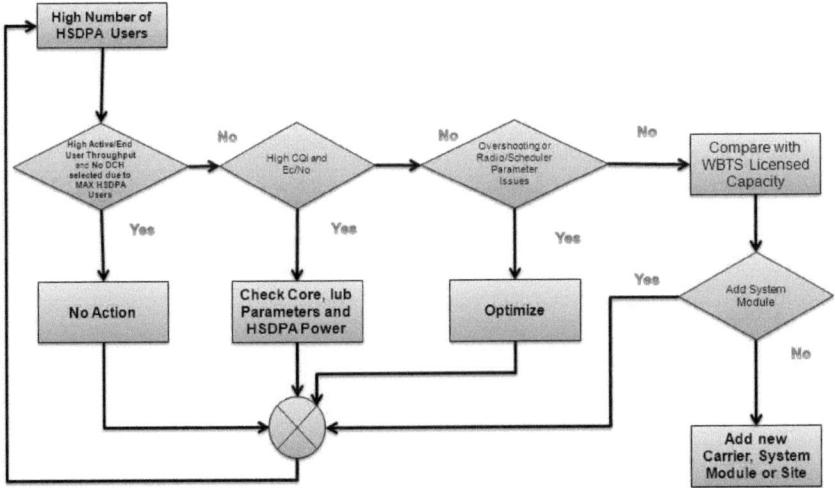

Figure 22: HSDPA Users Optimization

4.2.8   HSDPA Active/End User throughput

Throughput is the amount of user data bits transferred from the network to the UE. It is measured in units of bits/second (bps). In HSDPA throughput is usually measured at the MAC-d layer. For a discussion on layer protocol of HSDPA please refer to a guide on *HSDPA/UMTS or 3GPP*.

It is not meaningful to take the net HSDPA throughput as there might be users with no data in the buffers. This will decrease the overall throughput. It is beneficial to the look at HSDPA throughput both from network and user perspective.

The HSDPA throughput from network perspective is usually measured at MAC-d layer and is called, "**Active HSDPA MAC-d Throughput**". The throughput from the subscriber/User perspective is called, "**HSDPA End User Throughput**".

Active HSDPA MAC-d Throughput refers to the throughput when in each TTI some data was transferred to the UEs. This essentially provides us with an insight on the throughput from the MAC-d layer (Network perspective).

HSDPA End User Throughput is the average throughput experienced by a user on HS-DSCH. This is calculated by dividing the received data by the average number of users per TTI.

Low throughput seen from any of the above KPIs can be an indication of congestion on the numerous factors that affect HSDPA.

The following provides some generic areas that should be considered if such limitations are experienced in a live network:

4.2.8.1   Indications

1. Low HSDPA Active/End User Throughput
2. Low CQI and Ec/No
3. High Number of HSDPA Users
4. DCH selected to maximum HSDPA users

4.2.8.2   Resolution

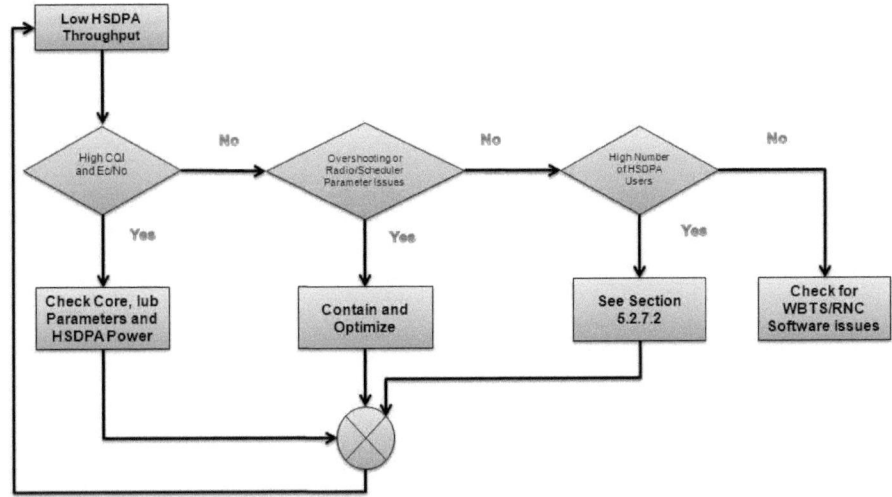

Figure 23: Low Throughput optimization

The parameters that can be considered for retuning can be:

Power Parameters: *PtxMaxHSDPA, PtxOffsetHSDPA, PtxTargetHSDPA, PtxTargetPS, PtxCellMax*
HSDPA Code Set: The maximum code set allowed for each user i.e. 5, 8, 10, 15 etc. and its associated timers.
DPCH over HSPDSCH: Increase the number of codes that cannot be preempted by NRT DPCH, if there is no DPCH congestion in the cell.
HSDPA H-ARQ: Parameters for algorithm used for H-ARQ can be changed.
Timer for switch between DCH and HS-DSCH: Timers can be changed to switch traffic quicker to HSDPA for improved throughput.
CELL_DCH to CELL_FACH or CELL_PCH Parameters/Timers: These should be optimized so that HSDPA throughput to active users can be improved.

4.3   3G NODE B/WBTS

NODE B or WBTS completes the air interface; it provides connectivity to the network for the UEs over the air interface. It consists of antennas, transceivers and digital signal processing (DSPs) boards to receive/transmit, modulate/demodulate and process the information contained in the transmissions.

A network may consist of numerous Node Bs providing coverage and capacity to large areas. Each Node B has a certain intended/planned area, in which it is required to provide services. If the number of subscribers increase by an amount larger than the capacity handling capability of the Node B, then congestion or blocking may be experienced.

The following factors influence capacity in a Node B/WBTS:

4.3.1   Number of Channel Elements (CEs)

Channel Elements (CEs) are DSP units located in the Node B. They are used for processing of R99 and HSPA services.

Different services (R99 RT, R99 NRT, HSDPA/HSUPA) require different processing powers and utilize different amount of CEs. Usually RT R99 uses one CE in DL and one in UL.

HSDPA and HSUPA CE capacity is usually reserved in the Node B and it is not available to other services.

CE utilization monitoring for R99 is straightforward - as the CE capacity reaches near 80% the CEs should be upgraded.

For HSDPA/HSUPA it is complicated due to different implementations by each OEM vendor. OEM vendors usually provide counters to compare the utilized capacity against the licensed capacity and upgrade decisions should be based on that. In addition the number of users of HSDPA and HSUPA for some OEM vendors is also limited by licenses, therefore these should be monitored as well and upgraded if congestion is attributed to capacity in the BTS.

4.3.1.1   Indications

1. High R99 CE Utilization
2. High HSDPA/HSUPA Number of Users than allowed/licensed
3. High Access Failures due to Node B
4. Low Throughput

4.3.1.2   Resolution

1. Add more licenses to activate more CEs
2. Add additional system modules/CEs
3. Add new layer or carrier

4.3.2   Control Plane Load

The Node B handles protocol stack NBAP which handles the signaling control between the RNC and the Node B.

The NBAP is further divided into C-NBAP (Common-NBAP) and D-NBAP (Dedicated-NBAP). C-NBAP controls signaling related to common channels setting up Radio Links etc.

D-NBAP is required for dedicated channel handling and Radio Link re-configuration etc.

Certain signaling units within the Node B are specific to an OEM vendor and documentation should always be consulted before upgrade decisions are made.

4.3.2.1 Indications

1. High Processor Load
2. RL rejections due to Processor Load

4.3.2.2 Resolution

1. Add more hardware

4.3.3 Number of Cells/Layer

A typical cell site will have one or more sectors. A Node B is divided into cells/sectors to increase gain using directional antennas and provide more capacity with another scrambling code.

Furthermore each separate frequency band available to the operator will be added as a new cell/layer to the Node B. e.g. adding 2100 layer to increase capacity.

Multiple layers can be added to a cell provided enough frequency band is available to the operator.

Each new cell/layer will increase capacity and coverage in a particular, pre-defined direction. Therefore with proper planning congestion in a certain area can be relieved by adding more cells/layers.

A typical three sectored site is shown below:

Figure 24: 3 Sectored Site

4.3.3.1 Indications

1. Congestion seen in a cell/layer on a Node B

4.3.3.2 Resolution

Add new layer/cells.

4.4   Iub Capacity

Iub is the interface between the Node B/WBTS and the RNC. It provides both user plane and control plane connectivity for the Node B to the RNC.

It should be noted that this guide assumes an IP-based Iub interface, while describing capacity limitations. For an ATM-based Iub, refer to the OEM vendor documentation.

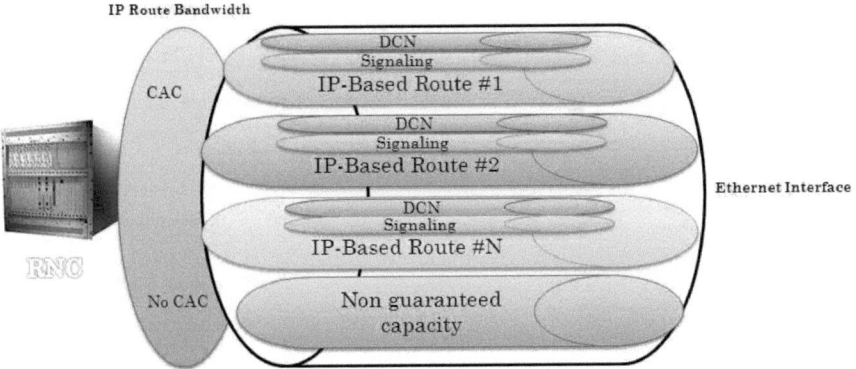

Figure 25: Example of IP Bandwidth Allocation

As can be seen from above there are two types of IP-Based Bandwidths - CAC and Non-CAC. Certain services require committed or guaranteed bandwidth and are subjected to Admission Control on the Iub. These services/bearers use the CAC bandwidth. For other services not requiring stringent Admission control Non-CAC bandwidth is utilized.

The IP-Based Iub Capacity can be monitored using the following:

4.4.1   IP-Based Route Bandwidth/Ethernet Bandwidth

This is either the total bandwidth of the IP-based Route or if Internal Flow Control is enabled it is the total available bandwidth of the Ethernet interface.

If the average throughput is more than the IP-Based Route Bandwidth then the interface will start dropping packets and needs to be upgraded.

Congestion in the IP-Route can result in lower throughputs if upgrades of the bandwidth are not carried out.

The congestion should be monitored using KPIs like Outgoing traffic volume, Incoming traffic volume, Ethernet port utilization for TX and RX etc.

4.4.1.1   Indications

1. High Incoming/Outgoing Data Volume on Iub
2. High throughput compared to bandwidth
3. Packet/Frame Loss due to Iub

4. Packet delays
5. HS-DSCH Credit Reductions

4.4.1.2   Resolution

Upgrade IP Bandwidth

4.4.2   IP-Based CAC Bandwidth

IP-Based CAC bandwidth is required for services like RT CS Voice and RT Streaming PS services.

This reserved bandwidth should be monitored to avoid blocking of the IP CAC. The IP CAC utilization should be monitored and if it exceeds 90% utilization more bandwidth should be reserved for CAC – provided if more bandwidth is available on the IP Route.

4.4.2.1   Indications

1. High Incoming/Outgoing Data Volume on Iub
2. Low accessibility ratio of IP Route for Incoming/Outgoing traffic
3. Failures due to Admission control

4.4.2.2   Resolution

Reserve more bandwidth for CAC traffic

4.5 RNC Capacity

Radio Network controller forms the brain of the Radio Access Network for 3G/UMTS. It interfaces to the Core Network on one side and to the UTRAN on the other side.

The RNC also contains Digital Signal processors for processing user and control plane information. In essence the RNC performs the following functions:

1. Controlling Node Bs connected to it
2. Iub Transport Resource Control
3. Power Control
4. Admission Control
5. Soft Handover Control and Radio Link Combining
6. Common Channel Management
7. Allocation of DL Channelization Codes etc.

The RNC capacity study comprises of monitoring capacity on the DSPs. Although in some manufacturers the number of users/Node Bs connected to the RNC maybe dependent on the software licenses allocated to the RNC.

It should be noted here that the RNC capacity is OEM vendor specific and each manufacturer have their own proprietary hardware design therefore, this should only be used as a guideline and proper manufacturer documentation should be obtained to analyze RNC capacity.

RNC Capacity is affected by the following:

4.5.1 RNC User Plane Processing Capacity

The RNC usually has a matrix of DSPs to handle the user plane processing. With each new user requesting a new service DSP resource utilization increases. The manufacturer may also define a limit for the number of users in CELL_DCH and CELL_FACH states.

The DSP load should be monitored for the RNC and upgrades should be planned when 70% utilization is exceeded, otherwise the service to the subscribers will be substandard as the RNC will start decreasing throughputs and downgrading radio bearers.

RRC Connected/Active Users: Each subscriber in RRC Connected mode will increase the load on the DSPs. These numbers can be calculated from the performance metrics available from the OEM vendor and should be compared to the maximum capacity of the User plane and upgrades planned accordingly.

4.5.1.1 Indications

1. High DSP Load
2. High DSP allocation failures
3. High number of users in CELL_DCH and CELL_FACH

4.5.1.2 Resolution

Upgrade RNC according to OEM vendor specifications

4.5.2 RNC Control plane/Signalling Handling Capacity

Control plane functions are handled by a different DSP unit (depending on the OEM vendor) in the RNC and it handles protocols like, NBAP, RANAP, RNSAP etc.

Overload of this unit can lead to severe performance degradations where access is denied to the network. Therefore loads on these units should be monitored proactively.

The overload on the unit can be caused by incorrect dimensioning, subscriber behavior, high paging etc.

The overload indications and possible resolution is provided below:

4.5.2.1 Indications

1. High Signaling unit Load
2. RRC Connection Setup Rejects
3. High deleted paging messages due to unit overload

4.5.2.2 Resolution

1. Enable Common Channel RRC Setup
2. Optimize for Event 1A/1B/1C
3. Disable RRC Connection Re-establishment
4. Upgrade according to OEM vendor specifications

4.5.3 Operations and Maintenance Unit (OMU) Capacity

OMU provides functionality to configure the network. It allows for maintenance functions such as hardware configuration, alarm monitoring, software upgrade etc.

The overload of this unit can be caused by too much maintenance activity. It is also used to transfer Performance metrics from the RNC to the Server and an overload will result in delay or no transfer of measurements at all.

Therefore, load on the OMU should also be monitored proactively.

4.5.3.1 Indications

1. High OMU load

4.5.3.2 Resolution

1. Upgrade according to OEM vendor specifications or escalate to O&M for review

4.5.4 Number of Cells/Carriers

The number of cells/carriers connected to an RNC is license limited for some OEM vendors. In such cases total number of cells connected to the RNC vs. license number should be compared.

4.5.4.1 *Indications*

1. High number of cells

4.5.4.2 *Resolution*

1. Add more licenses

5 REFERENCES

[1]   H. Holma and A. Toskala, WCDMA for UMTS, John Wiley, 2004.

[2]   T. HALONEN, GSM, GPRS and EDGE PERFORMANCE, John Wiley, 2003.

[3]   G. Heine, GSM Network: Protocols, Terminology, and Implementation, Artech House, 1998.

[4]   Nokia Siements Networks, "WCDMA RAN and I-HSPA, Rel. RU30, Operating Documentation, Issue 05," Nokia Siemens Networks, 2010.

[5]   Nokia Siements Networks, "GSM/EDGE BSS, Rel. RG20(BSS), Operating Documentation, Issue 05," 2010.

[6]   J. P. Romero, Radio Resource Management Strategies in UMTS, John Wiley, 2005.

[7]   3GPP Technical Specification 25.213, Spreading and Modulation (FDD), 3GPP.

[8]   3GPP Technical Specification 25.212, Multiplexing and Channel Coding (FDD), 3GPP.

[9]   3GPP Technical Specification 25.211, Physical Channels and Mapping of Transport Channels onto Physical Channels (FDD), 3GPP.

[10] 3GPP Technical Specification 25.214, Physical Layer Procedures (FDD), 3GPP.

[11] 3GPP Technical Specification 25.302, Services Provided by the Physical Layer, 3GPP.

[12] 3GPP Technical Specification 25.101, UE Radio Transmission and Reception (FDD), 3GPP.